Encyclopedia of
EARLY PEOPLES

By Richard C. Lawrence

CELEBRATION PRESS
Pearson Learning Group

The following people from **Pearson Learning Group**
have contributed to the development of this product:

Dorothea Fox, Joan Mazzeo **Design** | **Editorial** Leslie Feierstone-Barna, Cindy Kane
Christine Fleming **Marketing** | **Publishing Operations** Jennifer Van Der Heide
Production Laura Benford-Sullivan
Content Area Consultant Amy Keller

The following people from **DK** have
contributed to the development of this product:

Art Director Rachael Foster

Martin Wilson **Managing Art Editor** | **Managing Editor** Marie Greenwood
Polly Appleton **Design** | **Editorial** Selina Wood
Brenda Clynch **Picture Research** | **Production** Gordana Simakovic
Richard Czapnik, Andy Smith **Cover Design** | **DTP** David McDonald
Consultant: Philip Wilkinson

Dorling Kindersley would like to thank: Rose Horridge, Hayley Smith, and Gemma Woodward in the DK Picture Library;
Simon Mumford for cartography; Penny Smith for editorial assistance; Johnny Pau for additional cover design work.

Picture Credits: AKG London: 3b, 4t, 7b, 13bl, 14-15, 25br, 26tl, 28tc, 36tl; Erich Lessing 13tl; Dirk Radzinski 22b. Ancient Art & Architecture
Collection: 3cra, 11tl, 11b, 17b, 27br; Cheryl Hogue 5tc; Mike Maidment 36cl; R. Sheridan 31b, 32tl, 34-35b, 35br, 39; Gianni Tortilli 9tl.
Bridgeman Art Library, London/New York: 19tr; Alinari 18br; Bonhams, London, UK 5cl; People's Republic of China 15tr. Corbis: Christie's Images
23t; Penny Tweedie 4b. DK Images: American Museum of Natural History 17tr, 21b; British Museum 8cl, 10cl, 26bc, 30bl, 32bl, 35tr, 37bc, 37t;
© CONACULTA-INAH-MEX. Authorized reproduction by the Instituto Nacional de Antropologia e Historia 24tl, 25bl, 38tr, 38cl; Exeter Maritime
Museum 6tl; Pitt Rivers Museum 32-33b; University Museum of Archaeology and Anthropology, Cambridge 19b. Mary Evans Picture Library: 8br,
13cr. Werner Forman Archive: 5bcr, 6b, 24b, 26cr; British Museum, London 10br, 31tl; Courtesy David Bernstein Gallery, New York 18cl; Courtesy
Entwistle Gallery, London 1cbr, 30tl; Dallas Museum of Art, USA 30cr; Maxwell Museum of Anthropology, Albuquerque 27cla. Photo Scala, Florence:
Smithsonian Art Museum 28b. Top Topham: British Library 16t; The British Museum 1ca, 22tr; Charles Walker 29.
Jacket: Ancient Art & Architecture Collection: C. Boulanger front cr. Bridgeman Art Library, London/New York: People's Republic of China back.
DK Images: © CONACULTA-INAH-MEX. Authorized reproduction by the Instituto Nacional de Antropologia e Historia front l; Museum of London
front tr; Museum of Mankind front bc, front ca; University Museum of Archaeology and Anthropology, Cambridge front c.

All other images: Dorling Kindersley © 2005. For further information see www.dkimages.com

ISBN: 0-7652-5262-7

Color reproduction by Colourscan, Singapore
Printed in the United States of America
2 3 4 5 6 7 8 9 10   08 07 06 05

1-800-321-3106
www.pearsonlearning.com

Introduction

The word *people* refers to a group of human beings who share a **culture**. Usually, these people live in a specific place and share the same language and customs.

Most researchers believe that the first peoples evolved more than 100,000 years ago in Africa. By about 11,000 years ago, humans were living on every continent except Antarctica. Because these people were among the first to live in their particular locality, they are often called early peoples. Some, like the Maori of New Zealand, still live in the lands they originally settled. Others, such as the Saxons, have **assimilated**, mixing their bloodlines, languages, and cultures with those of other peoples.

This encyclopedia explores these early peoples. The boldface words within the body of the text appear in the glossary. Words that appear in all capital letters signal a cross-reference, a listing in which to look for additional information.

part of a Saxon buckle

Etruscan painting showing a servant and musicians

Aa
Bb
Cc
Dd
Ee
Ff
Gg
Hh
Ii
Jj
Kk
Ll
Mm
Nn
Oo
Pp
Qq
Rr
Ss
Tt
Uu
Vv
Ww
Xx
Yy
Zz

Aa

Abbasids

illustration from a story by Abbasid philosopher and poet Hariri

The Abbasid **dynasty** ruled the Islamic Empire from A.D. 750 to 1258. The Abbasids moved the capital city from Damascus to Baghdad in A.D. 762. Under the rule of Harun al-Rashid and his son, al-Mamum, Baghdad became a great center of art and learning in the 700s and 800s A.D. Today, Baghdad is the capital of Iraq. Abbasid rule ended when Baghdad fell to the MONGOLS in 1258.

Aboriginal Australians

Aboriginal Australians were the first people to live in Australia. More than 60,000 years ago, they crossed a land bridge from Asia to settle in Australia. They created multi-use tools such as the boomerang, the digging stick, and the spear thrower. Some Aboriginal Australians were **nomads**, moving from place to place to find food and water. They developed a strong belief system based on the Dreamtime, a time at the beginning of Earth. Many Aboriginal Australians carry on these beliefs through stories, music, and art.

The British settlement of Australia, beginning in 1788, cost Aboriginal Australians much of their land. Many were killed by violence and disease. Since the 1970s, government policies have gradually recognized Aboriginal rights. Today, Aboriginal peoples number about 410,000, or 2 percent of Australia's population.

Aboriginal Australians using body paint in preparation for a ceremony

Adena

stone pestle for grinding corn, used by the Adena people

This ancient Native American culture existed from about 500 B.C. to A.D. 100, in and around what is now southern Ohio, in the United States. Historians named this group of people the Adena after the Ohio town where **artifacts** created by these people were found. Adena people lived in round houses made of wood and bark. They buried their dead in large mounds in which many finely crafted artifacts have been found.

Ainu

Ainu depiction of men with sledges and dogs

While historians are unsure of where the Ainu came from or when they arrived, this group of people has lived in the islands of present-day Japan for thousands of years. As hunters, fishermen, and trappers, the Ainu lived in villages along rivers and near game trails. Ainu culture reached its peak in the thirteenth century, when they lived on all four of the major islands of Japan. From the fifteenth century, the Ainu were forced out of their lands and made to assimilate into the Japanese population. Today, a small number of Ainu live on the Japanese island of Hokkaido, as well as on Sakhalin Island.

Aksumites

Kingdom of Aksum

ASIA

AFRICA

Egypt • Memphis

Nile River

Red Sea

Arabian Peninsula

A F R I C A

Adulis

Aksum

Gulf of Aden

INDIAN OCEAN

KEY

heartland of Aksumite kingdom

extent of Aksumite kingdom

0 miles 800
0 kilometers 800

This map shows the extent of the Aksum kingdom during the height of its influence (first to seventh century A.D.).

Aksum was a powerful kingdom in what is now northern Ethiopia, from about A.D. 50 to 600. It was a well-known trade center during ROMAN times. The graves of wealthy Aksumites were marked by huge stone obelisks, some of which are still standing. Aksum lost power in the 900s A.D., but its culture continued in Ethiopia.

Aksumite obelisk still standing in the town of Axum, Ethiopia

model of an Algonquin canoe

Algonquins

When Europeans arrived in North America in the 1500s, this group of Native Americans inhabited areas of what are now southeast Canada and the northeastern United States. They made **wigwams** and clothes of animal skins, and winter homes covered with birch bark. They used canoes, toboggans, and snowshoes for travel. In the late 1600s, the Algonquins were constantly at war with the IROQUOIS, fighting over territory and control of the fur trade. This, plus diseases such as measles and smallpox, reduced their population greatly. Today, several thousand Algonquins live in Ontario and Quebec.

Anasazi

This group of southwest Native Americans were farming, weaving, and pottery-making peoples. They flourished in what is now the western and southwestern United States, including parts of Arizona, New Mexico, Colorado, and Utah, between A.D. 100 and 1300. They built multistory dwellings, beginning about A.D. 700. Then, about 1200, they began to build apartment villages on cliff faces. These villages, which were made of stone or **adobe**, were two to four stories high and contained 20 to 1,000 rooms. The dwellings were mysteriously abandoned around the 1300s. These people are the ancestors of the Pueblos and Hopis, who prefer to call them Hisatsinom.

ruins of Anasazi cliff-dwellings at Mesa Verde, Colorado

Assyrians

This ancient group of people lived in northern **Mesopotamia**, which today is part of Iraq and Syria. They were feared as warriors. Beginning in the thirteenth century B.C., the Assyrians conquered several independent states. By the ninth century B.C., they ruled over a powerful kingdom. The kingdom ended with the destruction of the city of Nineveh by the BABYLONIANS and MEDES in 612 B.C.

Assyrian horse sculpture made of bronze

Aztecs

The Aztecs ruled an empire that began around 1325. They settled on islands in Lake Texcoco, where Mexico City now stands. Here they founded Tenochtitlán, their capital. Tenochtitlán was a beautiful city crisscrossed by canoe-filled canals, with **pyramid** temples at the center. Its parks, zoos, and markets amazed visitors. The Aztec Empire grew to include more than 400 small states and more than 5 million people. Aztec wealth came from agriculture. The Aztecs' central government promoted education, taxation, and law enforcement. The empire was still expanding when, in 1519, Spanish soldiers destroyed the capital city and imprisoned the Aztec king. The Spanish then made this area into a colony of Spain.

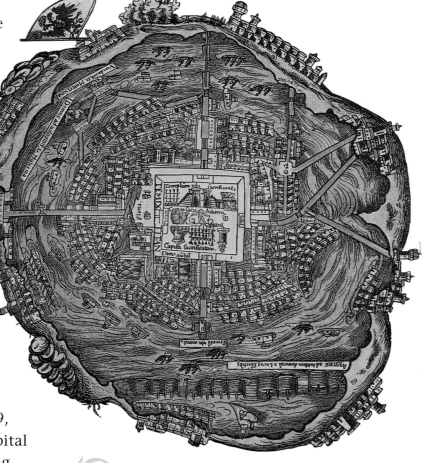

The Aztec capital of Tenochtitlán covered 5 square miles. This map, made by the Spanish, dates from 1524.

Bb

Babylonians

Babylonian clay tablet depicting the world and the universe

Babylonians ruled an empire on the Euphrates River in Mesopotamia. The empire began about 1900 B.C., when a desert people called the Amorites conquered the area and founded a dynasty. Their sixth king, Hammurabi (ruled 1792–1750 B.C.), extended his power into Persia and Anatolia, now eastern Turkey. Hammurabi is famous for developing an ancient set of laws called Hammurabi's Code. During the centuries that followed, Babylon, the capital city of Babylonia, fell into the hands of several foreign kingdoms. Eventually, the Babylonians regained their independence.

In the seventh century B.C., under the rule of King Nebuchadnezzar II, Babylon became one of the greatest cities in the world. Historians believe that the Babylonians invented the 60-minute hour.

Bantus

Bantus are an African people who most likely originated in what is now Cameroon, about 2,000 years ago. They were farmers who made iron tools and weapons. Over time, they migrated south into central and southern Africa, spreading their language and possibly their knowledge of ironwork. Today, there are more than 180 million people descended from the Bantu people, belonging to about 300 different cultures, including Zulu, SHONA, and Tango. However, because their cultures are now so different, Bantu today refers to a group of similar languages, not to a distinct people.

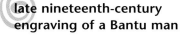

late nineteenth-century engraving of a Bantu man

8

Berbers

The Berbers have lived in North Africa since around 3000 B.C. By the second century B.C., they became a threat to the ROMANS. From the eleventh to the thirteenth centuries A.D., their control extended into the northwestern part of Africa and into Spain. Today, there are about 15 million Berbers. Their traditional culture of herding and farming survives today, mainly in mountain villages and desert areas of Libya, Algeria, and Morocco.

Berber women in front of their home in Sakket, Tunisia

Byzantines

Byzantines were the people of the eastern half of the ROMAN Empire. Emperor Constantine set up a capital at Byzantium in A.D. 330, renaming it Constantinople. (It is now Istanbul, Turkey.) After the fall of Rome in A.D. 476, the western half of the Roman Empire lost its power. Yet the Byzantine Empire lasted 1,000 years more. Emperor Justinian I (ruled A.D. 527–565) reasserted control over Italy and North Africa and compiled a set of laws. These laws, the Justinian Code, shaped modern European law.

Byzantine mosaic floor in a church in Jordan

The Byzantine Empire enjoyed a golden age of art and literature from A.D. 867 to 1081. Over the next four centuries, the Byzantine Empire was gradually taken over by the Turks, who captured Constantinople in 1453 and made it the capital of their Ottoman Empire.

This map shows the extent of the Byzantine Empire under Justinian I (A.D. 527–565).

EUROPE
Danube River
Black Sea
Rome
Constantinople
Athens
Antioch
Carthage
Mediterranean Sea
ASIA
Alexandria
Nile River
The Byzantine Empire
0 miles 800
0 kilometers 800
AFRICA

Cc

Canaanites

Canaanite necklace

Canaanites lived in ancient Palestine, land that is now part of Israel and Jordan. The Canaanites lived in small **city-states** ruled by local kings. Many believe the Canaanites were the first people to use an alphabet. The HEBREWS conquered Palestine around 1250 B.C. By the eighth century B.C., the Canaanites were most likely assimilated into the Hebrew civilization.

Celts

The Celts are the ancestors of many Europeans. The earliest evidence of their existence places them in present-day Germany around 700 B.C. By 300 B.C., the Celts had settled much of western and southern Europe. Most Celts grew wheat and raised livestock. They were also one of the first peoples to use iron, and their burials often included chariots and weapons. The Celts developed a style of art that included elaborate patterns of curves. They had no writing system. Instead, they passed on information and history verbally, through poetry reciting and conversation.

Although Celtic culture dominated northwest Europe for several hundred years, Celtic tribes never formed a unified nation. By A.D. 100, the ROMANS had conquered most of Europe. Celtic culture remained only in southwest England and some areas of Ireland, Scotland, Wales, and northwest France. Even then, this culture blended with other cultures, and its people were assimilated.

This bronze shield with red glass inlays shows the many curves typical of Celtic art.

stone figurine, typical of the Chavín people

Chimú

The Chimú lived in Peru beginning in about 1200. They irrigated fields, built cities, and worked with metal and fabric. Their style of pottery is distinct. Their capital, Chan, contained 6 to 10 square miles of rectangular streets, walls, reservoirs, and temples, all created with adobe. Between 1465 and 1470, the INCAS conquered the Chimú. Much of Chimú culture was then absorbed by the Incas.

Chimú pottery, with its distinctive dark glazing

Chavín

This first civilization of Peru flourished between about 900 and 200 B.C. The Chavíns created an economy based on agriculture. Their modern ways of farming allowed them to successfully grow crops.

Cholas

This dynasty ruled in southern India for several hundred years until 1279. Cholas valued literature and built great temples and monuments. Their villages were self-governed.

The magnificent Brihadishvara Temple was built by the Cholas in the eleventh century.

Ee

Egyptians, Ancient

Key Dates

3100 B.C.
Upper and Lower Egypt are unified under one ruler.

2680–2565 B.C.
The Pyramids of Giza are built.

About 2600–2100 B.C.
Old Kingdom; rulers built pyramids as burial sites.

2040–1792 B.C.
Middle Kingdom; Egypt's power expands.

1570–1070 B.C.
New Kingdom; the empire reaches its height.

1070 B.C.
The period of decline begins.

Ancient Egypt was one of the most advanced civilizations of its time. Ancient Egyptians lived in the valley of the Nile River from about 3200 B.C. They learned how to use the Nile's flooding to **irrigate**, or provide water for, their crops.

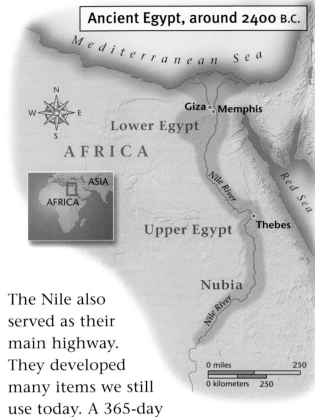

Ancient Egypt, around 2400 B.C.

Mediterranean Sea

Giza · Memphis

Lower Egypt

AFRICA

ASIA
AFRICA

Nile River

Red Sea

Upper Egypt · Thebes

Nubia

Nile River

0 miles 250
0 kilometers 250

The Nile also served as their main highway. They developed many items we still use today. A 365-day calendar and a base-ten number system are just two examples. The ancient Egyptians were also one of the first civilizations to use writing. About 3000 B.C., they began to write in **hieroglyphs**, or picture writing. They are also known for building great pyramids in which they buried their pharaohs, or kings. Scientists today are not sure exactly how they built these architectural wonders without modern tools. Egypt's power declined after about 1070 B.C., but its civilization continued to influence those of the ancient GREEKS, NUBIANS, ROMANS, and PERSIANS. Many of its artifacts and pyramids can still be seen today.

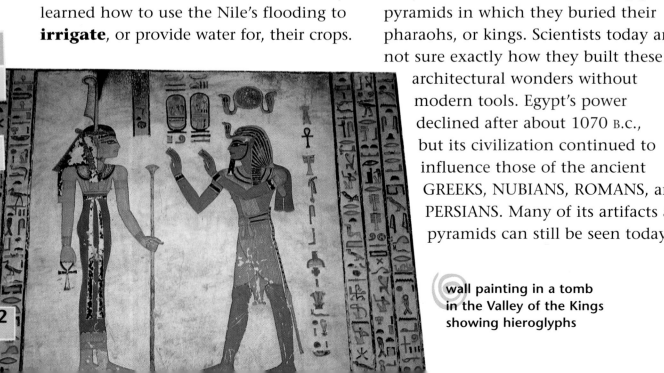

wall painting in a tomb in the Valley of the Kings showing hieroglyphs

Elamite cuneiform writing listing trade words, such as words for metals, oils, and foods

Elamites

Elamites lived in what is now southwestern Iran from about 5000 to 1100 B.C. They adopted **cuneiform** writing from the Akkadian people of Babylonia. The Elamites had a matrilinear ruling system. This meant that the next ruler was always the "son of a sister" in the ruler's family. The BABYLONIANS defeated the Elamites in the 1100s B.C.

Etruscans

Etruscan civilization thrived in what is now northern Italy, between 800 and 600 B.C. The Etruscans are credited with inventing the toga and the first cosmetic dentistry. They greatly influenced the ROMANS, who conquered them between 300 and 200 B.C.

Etruscan tomb wall painting showing dancers

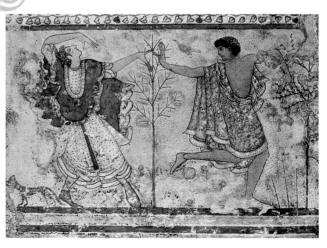

Ff

Franks

nineteenth-century depiction of a Frankish warrior

The Franks were a Germanic people living on the east side of the Rhine River in the third century A.D. Under the leadership of Clovis and his **successors**, the Franks expanded their kingdom to what are now Belgium, northern France, and western Germany. During this expansion, the ROMANS influenced Frankish culture. The culture that grew from the combination of these two peoples helped create today's cultures of western Europe.

Gg

Greeks, Ancient

Key Dates

About 3000 B.C.
Minoan culture begins on island of Crete.

About 2000 B.C.
Mainland is settled by peoples from the north.

1600 B.C.
Mycenaean civilization begins.

700s B.C.
Athens and Sparta are prominent city-states.

400s B.C.
Golden age of Athens; Athenians defeat Persians in Persian Wars.

431 B.C.
Sparta defeats Athens in Peloponnesian War.

338 B.C.
Philip II of Macedonia defeats southern city-states.

323 B.C.
Death of Alexander the Great.

146 B.C.
Conquest of Greece by Rome.

A.D. 395
Greece becomes part of eastern Roman Empire, which becomes Byzantine Empire.

This ancient people built an amazing civilization in Greece between about 750 B.C. and 323 B.C. They made great contributions to philosophy, drama, science, and mathematics. They also held the first Olympic games in 776 B.C. Ancient Greek civilization reached its height in the fifth century B.C., after it fought off an invasion by the PERSIANS.

Ancient Greece, around 700 B.C.

0 miles 800
0 kilometers 800

Macedonia
Mount Olympus
Thessaly
Aegean Sea
Troy
Greece
Asia Minor
Ionian Sea
Athens
Olympia
Mycenae
Peloponnesus
Sparta
Crete
Knossos
Mediterranean Sea

Greece was made up of many independently run city-states, each with its own government. The city-state of Athens was the first to develop democracy as a form of government. Eventually, fighting between city-states weakened them, making it possible for Alexander the Great from Macedonia to unify Macedonia and Greece. Alexander the Great then built Greece into an empire stretching from Egypt to India. Although the empire crumbled after Alexander's death, Greek civilization continued to influence the Western world, especially the ancient ROMANS.

Scholars believe that the blind poet Homer wrote two of the world's greatest epic poems, the *Iliad* and the *Odyssey*. These poems are exciting stories of adventure that are still popular today.

Hh

Han

The Han dynasty (206 B.C. to A.D. 220) lasted longer than any other Chinese dynasty. It became the model for all the dynasties that followed it.

The Han dynasty was established by Liu Pang, a farmer who led a revolt against the previous dynasty, the Ch'in dynasty. During the Han dynasty, the Chinese empire expanded greatly. Chinese culture also flourished. Writing became common, and the Han wrote books on history, philosophy, mathematics, and medicine. They composed poetry and created the first dictionary. They also developed an extensive education system.

Han terra-cotta figure of a horseman

The Han dynasty also gave rise to several scientific and technological advances. The Han developed porcelain, measured time with sundials and water clocks, and even invented a tool to measure the force of earthquakes. Silk weaving became a major industry, and the Han traded extensively with their neighbors. They built huge palaces and tombs. Han emperors often filled their tombs with terra-cotta statues of men and horses.

This fourteenth-century illustration shows the Hebrews crossing the Red Sea with the Egyptians in pursuit.

Hebrews

The Hebrew people settled in tribes in Canaan, in the Middle East, about 1800 B.C. Around 1000 B.C., King David united the Hebrews and founded the kingdom of Israel. Israel divided into two kingdoms around 900 B.C., and both were subsequently conquered by different invaders. The Hebrew Bible is the basis of Judaism, one of the earliest **monotheistic** religions, and the Hebrews are the ancestors of modern Jewish people.

This is the world's first known peace treaty, the Treaty of Kadesh between the Hittites and Egyptians.

Hittites

The Hittites were perhaps the first people to use iron weapons. They gained power in the Middle East before the ASSYRIANS or the BABYLONIANS. Their empire flourished from about 1400 to 1200 B.C. Around 1299 B.C. at Kadesh, in Syria, the Hittites fought against the ancient EGYPTIANS. Sixteen years later, the two empires made the world's first known peace treaty. Little is known about the collapse of the Hittites. Scholars think that a mass movement of people in the Middle East may have contributed to their decline.

Hohokam

From 300 B.C. to A.D. 1400, Hohokam people lived in what is now Arizona, in the southwestern United States. They are possibly the ancestors of the Native American groups the Pimas (Akimel O'odham) and the Papagos (Tohono O'odham). The Hohokam were the greatest irrigation engineers of the ancient Americas. They used their watering system to grow **maize**, cotton, beans, and squash.

The Hohokam built a 3-mile canal from the Gila River before A.D. 500. By the fourteenth century, they had constructed more than 150 miles of canals. Some of the canals were restored for use in the twentieth century.

Sometime after 1100, the Hohokam encountered the Salado people, a branch of the ANASAZI. From them, the Hohokam learned to build multistory houses with adobe walls. Hohokam culture declined after about 1450. Historians are unsure why it disappeared.

traditional Hohokam pot

Hopewell

Hopewell culture flourished between 200 B.C. and A.D. 400, in what is now southern Ohio, in the north-central United States. Like the ADENA, these Native American people built huge burial mounds. Hopewell metalwork included copper, iron, gold, and silver, and often featured sheets of the mineral mica. The Hopewell people traded with peoples as far away as the Rocky Mountains, the Gulf of Mexico, and the Atlantic Ocean. Their culture weakened after about A.D. 400.

Hopewell burial mound

Huari

The Huari inhabited the Andes Mountains of what is now Peru, around A.D. 600–1000. A military power, they controlled much of the highlands and the coast of Peru. They built large, stone tombs for burial of their leaders and constructed temples decorated with human figures.

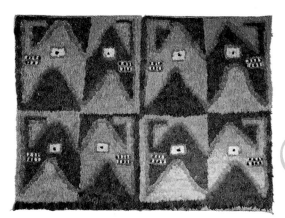

detail from a Huari featherwork tabbard with dragon-head motif

Early Peoples of the Andes Region

Ecuador

SOUTH AMERICA

Peru
Chile — Bolivia

Argentina

Chimú
A.D. 700–1470

Huari
about A.D. 600–1000

Chavin
900–200 B.C.

Nazca
about 200 B.C.–A.D. 600

Incas
about A.D. 1400–1532

PACIFIC OCEAN

Andes Mountains

N
W   E
S

0 miles   800
0 kilometers   800

This map shows some of the early peoples who lived in the Andes region of South America. Boundaries of present-day countries are shown.

Hun

The Huns were the most feared people of Europe during the fifth century A.D. Their superb archery skills made them excellent warriors. They began as nomads, wandering in Mongolia, central Asia, looking for food. They did not farm. Instead, they herded animals and robbed peoples they conquered. Around A.D. 432 their first king, Rugila, defeated the ROMANS in battle. Rugila's nephew, Attila, then attacked the eastern and central parts of the far-reaching Roman Empire. Attila collected great treasures of gold from his enemies. He then was able to establish a central government. After his death in A.D. 453, the people he conquered revolted and took back their lands.

fifteenth-century illustration of Atilla the Hun on horseback

Ii

Incas

The Incas ruled one of the largest empires of South America during the 1500s. Their empire stretched along the Andes Mountains on the west coast of South America.

A strong government held the empire together. The Incas built roads and hanging rope bridges. They also built an irrigation system to supply water to farms, which were built on terraces carved into the mountainsides. Their temple walls had huge stones cut to fit together without cement. The Inca Empire was destroyed by the Spanish, who arrived in 1532 in search of gold. Today, Incas still remain in some regions high in the Andes. People in villages there speak Quechua, the Inca language. Forty-five percent of Peruvians are descendants of the Incas.

Inca ruins at Machu Picchu, Peru

Indus

Indus civilization arose about 2500 B.C. near the Indus River, in what is now Pakistan and northwestern India. The Indus people built two cities, Harappa and Mohenjo-Daro. Like the ancient EGYPTIANS, they learned to use the rivers to irrigate their crops. They also developed a system of writing. Indus civilization faded by about 1750 B.C., possibly because of invasions.

Indus stone seal showing the image of a bull

Inuit boy and girl

Inuits

Inuits have lived in the far north of Canada, Alaska, Greenland, and Siberia for thousands of years. The Inuits are also known as Eskimos. Those who now live in Canada, Alaska, and Greenland are thought to have come originally from northeast Asia about 5000 years ago.

Traditionally, Inuits hunted seal, walrus, whale, polar bear, caribou (reindeer), and musk oxen. Inuit women sewed animal-skin clothing. The Inuits turned bone, antlers, horns, and teeth into tools, weapons, and works of art. Oil made from blubber (seal or whale fat) was used as lamp fuel. Inuits dwelled in skin tents in summer and sod houses in winter. They usually used snow houses, or igloos, only as temporary shelters. Transportation was by dogsled or boat— the small kayak and the larger *umiak*. Today, most Inuits live in wooden houses, wear modern clothing, and use snowmobiles.

Iroquois

The Iroquois are a group of Native American nations that banded together in the 1500s. They lived around what is now central New York, in the northeastern United States. Iroquois villages were made up of longhouses, which they constructed from timber and covered with bark. Each longhouse had separate living areas for individual families. The Iroquois were governed by a council of elected delegates. Women had high status, including the power to remove unpopular delegates and to choose replacements. The Iroquois exchanged **wampum** beads as a form of trade and also used them for communication. Fierce in battle, the Iroquois were often at war with other Native American peoples over land for trapping and agriculture. By 1700, they had severely weakened the Hurons and ALGONQUINS to their west. Today, more than 60,000 Iroquois live in the United States and Canada.

An Iroquois longhouse could be as large as 200 feet long and could hold twenty families.

Jj

Jomon

reconstruction of a Jomon house

The Jomon inhabited Japan from about 10,000 to 300 B.C. They lived in small villages, hunted deer and game, fished, and gathered nuts and berries. The Jomon made pottery, which they decorated with cord impressions.

Kk

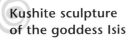

**Kushite sculpture
of the goddess Isis**

Khmers

The Khmers are the native people of Cambodia. From about A.D. 800 to 1434, the Khmer Empire was at its peak. It left outstanding sculpture and architecture, such as the temple complex Angkor Wat. In 1434, the Khmer capital, Angkor, was captured by the Thai. Today, most of the people of Cambodia consider themselves Khmers.

the ruins of Angkor Wat

Kushites

Also called Southern NUBIANS, Kushites lived along the Nile River and were ruled by the EGYPTIANS until about 800 B.C. At that time, they took control of Egypt. They later built the capital city of Meroë on the Nile River.

The city lay on an important trade route from Egypt to the Red Sea. Its surrounding hills were mined for gold and emeralds. This made the Kushites a very wealthy people. After the ASSYRIANS drove them out of Egypt, Kushite kings ruled Nubia for another 1,000 years. The Kushites even survived a ROMAN invasion. However, Kush fell to the AKSUMITES in the 300s A.D.

model of a Makah hunting canoe

Mm

Makahs

Makahs are a Native American people who have lived in northwestern Washington, in the northwestern United States, since at least A.D. 1000. They are known for their rich artistic culture and large feasts called potlatches. Makah society once had complex rankings. Each individual had a numbered place within a family. Because eating whale is traditional to their culture, today the Makahs are the only people in the United States who are allowed to hunt whales.

Maori

The Maori migrated from the POLYNESIAN islands to New Zealand around A.D. 800. Maori traditionally lived in tribes led by chiefs. A tribe was divided into subtribes, and then into extended families. Men fished, planted crops such as the sweet potato, and made wood carvings. Women gathered vegetables and shellfish, and wove flax into mats, garments, and bags. The Maori gathered in meeting houses decorated with carvings. There, they sang and made speeches. Today, the Maori make up about 15 percent of the population of New Zealand.

Maori demonstrating a traditional dance, joined by tourists

Maya pottery figurine of an important man wearing an ornate headdress, necklace, and large earplugs

Maya

The Maya built a great Central American civilization that reached its peak between A.D. 250 and 900. The Maya people began as farmers of maize, beans, squash, and chili peppers. By about A.D. 200, they had built cities with pyramids, palaces, and temples. Maya civilization at its height included 2 million people in forty cities. Maya architecture, sculpture, mathematics, astronomy, and writing were very advanced. The Maya wrote on paper made from the bark of fig trees. They invented a calendar and were able to predict solar eclipses.

Each Maya city had its own ruler, and cities often fought against one another. Maya cities began to decline around A.D. 900. No one is sure why. Many Maya ruins are still visible in the rain forests of southern Mexico, Guatemala, and Belize. About 2 million Maya, mostly farmers, still live in that region.

Medes

This southwest Asian people lived in Media, which is in modern-day Iran. By 836 B.C., they were ruled by the ASSYRIANS. Two centuries later, they rebelled and formed their own kingdom. The Medes, with the BABYLONIANS and SCYTHIANS, captured the Assyrian capital of Nineveh in 612 B.C. Then in 550 B.C., the Medes were conquered by the PERSIANS.

This carving on a staircase at the ancient Tripylon Palace, Iran, depicts a procession of Medes and Persians.

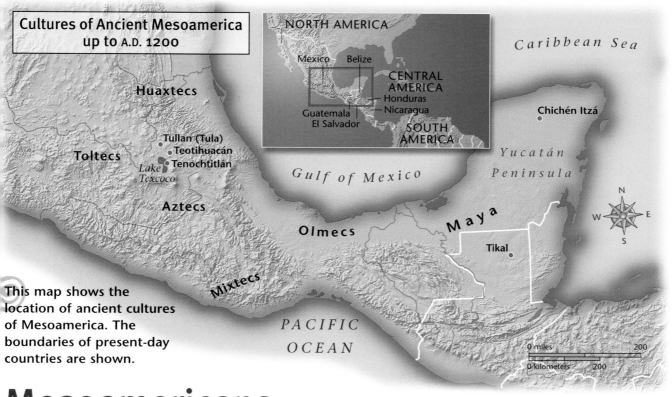

Cultures of Ancient Mesoamerica up to A.D. 1200

NORTH AMERICA

Mexico Belize

CENTRAL AMERICA
— Honduras
— Nicaragua
Guatemala
El Salvador
SOUTH AMERICA

Caribbean Sea

Huaxtecs

Tullan (Tula)
• Teotihuacán
Toltecs
Lake Texcoco • Tenochtitlán

Aztecs

Gulf of Mexico

Chichén Itzá

Yucatán Peninsula

Olmecs

M a y a

Tikal

Mixtecs

PACIFIC OCEAN

N
W   E
S

0 miles   200
0 kilometers   200

This map shows the location of ancient cultures of Mesoamerica. The boundaries of present-day countries are shown.

Mesoamericans

Mesoamerican is the name for a large grouping of ancient cultures that thrived in present-day Mexico and most of Central America. These civilizations included AZTECS, MAYA, OLMECS, TOLTECS, MIXTECS, and Huaxtecs.

The civilizations shared many traits and traditions. They had similar writing systems, large stone temples, sculpture, and pottery. They also played a ball game on a court shaped like a capital *I*.

In this game, players wore thick padding and tried to hit a small, hard, rubber ball through a high goal without using their hands or feet. They were allowed to use their hips, knees, and elbows. All of these cultures died out during Spanish colonization in the 1500s.

Mesoamerican sculpture of a ball player

Mesoamerican ball court at Chichén Itzá, Mexico

This fresco from the palace of Knossos shows the Minoan sport of bull-leaping.

Minoans

On the Mediterranean island of Crete, Minoans created the first known European civilization between 2000 and 1450 B.C. Information about their culture has been gathered from the ruins of their cities and palaces, especially the palace at Knossos. Minoan **fresco** paintings show important Minoan cultural symbols, such as bulls and dolphins. By about 1580 B.C., Minoan traders had spread across the Aegean Sea to Greece, where they influenced the MYCENAEANS and traded with the EGYPTIANS and Syrians. The Minoans were conquered by the Mycenaeans in the middle of the fifteenth century B.C.

Mississippians

Mississippians were a Native American farming culture. From about A.D. 800 to the mid-1500s, they lived along the Mississippi River, in what is now the central United States. They may have learned how to improve their ways of farming from MESOAMERICAN peoples. By 1000, Mississippian villages had formed city-states. Mississippians were experts in making a wide range of crafts, such as headdresses, masks, and pipes. War among the Mississippian groups led to the creation of walled towns. Mississippian culture declined after the arrival of European explorers.

mask worn by a Mississippian shaman

Mixtecs

Descendants of this MESOAMERICAN group still live in several southern Mexican states. Mixtec culture flourished between the ninth and early sixteenth centuries A.D. The Mixtecs have always been skilled at metalwork, pottery, weaving, stonework, and mosaics.

gold pendant made by the Mixtecs

Mogollon

The Mogollon were the first pottery-making people in what is now the southwestern United States, beginning about 200 B.C. They disappeared in the thirteenth century A.D. for unknown reasons.

Mogollon pottery bowl used in burial rituals

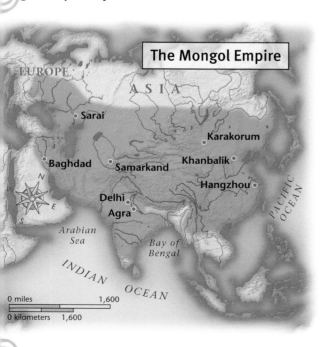

The Mongol Empire

EUROPE

ASIA

Sarai

Karakorum

Baghdad

Samarkand

Khanbalik

Hangzhou

Delhi

Agra

Arabian Sea

Bay of Bengal

INDIAN OCEAN

PACIFIC OCEAN

0 miles 1,600
0 kilometers 1,600

This map shows the Mongol Empire at its height in the late 1200s.

Mongols

The Mongols were tribes of nomadic shepherds who traveled with their flocks of cattle, sheep, goats, and horses around the grassy plains of central Asia for thousands of years. They lived in yurts, domed tents made of branches covered with hides or felt. Mongol society was based on extended families that were grouped together into clans. Sometimes clans banded together to fight common enemies, but at other times the clans fought against each other.

Early in the thirteenth century A.D., a fierce warrior named Temujin rose to power, united the Mongol clans, and greatly expanded the Mongol Empire. The Mongol clans named him Ghengis Khan, "ruler of the world," in 1206. He ruled over what was possibly the world's largest empire. The Mongol civilization reached its peak under Ghengis Khan's grandson Kublai, who became the great Khan in 1260. The empire declined later as, one by one, the different peoples conquered by the Mongols broke away.

Kublai Khan

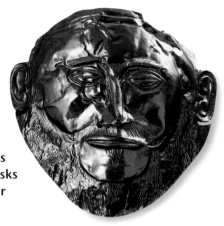

The Mycenaeans made burial masks of gold to honor their royalty.

Mycenaeans

These warriors from the mainland of present-day Greece became the major power in the Aegean Sea after conquering the MINOANS. Their existence was discovered through excavations at the site of the ancient city of Mycenae in Greece. Mycenaean cities were noted for their palaces, citadels, and fortresses. About 1450 B.C., they invaded the island of Crete. They took over Minoan palaces and trading routes, and absorbed Minoan art and writing into their own culture. The Mycenaeans produced fine bronze and gold metalwork, and built large tombs for their royalty.

Nn

Native Americans of the Plains

Thirty Native American nations lived in the grassland between the Rocky Mountains and the Mississippi River, in what is now the central United States. Most of the nations, such as the Comanches, Crows, Cheyennes, and Teton Sioux, were nomadic peoples who used bows and arrows to hunt buffalo and other big game. Meat, bones, hides, and horns provided food, tools, shelter, and clothing. In the eastern part of the plains, nations such as the Pawnees, Mandans, Hidatsas, and Arikaras also farmed maize, beans, squash, and sunflowers.

a Native American (Comanche) Village, 1834

Before the arrival of Europeans, Plains Native Americans hunted on foot by driving buffalo over a cliff or into a circle of fire. Buffalo hunting was revolutionized when the Native Americans acquired horses from the Spanish. However, with the arrival of European settlers, many things changed. Disease and war reduced the population of these nations. They were forced to move to reservations, which deprived them of their traditional means of support. Although many individuals adapted to a new way of life on the reservations, others did not. Today, whether living on or off reservations, many Native Americans still struggle to balance their traditional ways with life in modern times.

Nazca

The Nazca lived on the southern coast of present-day Peru from about 200 B.C. to A.D. 600. They wove beautiful textiles and made multicolored pottery with animal, plant, and human designs. However, they are best known for the Nazca Lines. These are about seventy enormous line drawings of animals, plants, and geometric shapes made on the dry plains near the modern-day city of Nazca. Their purpose or meaning is unknown.

an aerial image of a Nazca Line drawing depicting a monkey

Nok head made from clay

Nok

Nok culture thrived in Africa, in what is now Nigeria, between about 500 B.C. and A.D. 200. It is known for clay figurines of animals and humans, especially of human heads.

Nubians

Nubians inhabited what is now southern Egypt and Sudan. Nubian rulers were among the world's first kings. By 2950 B.C., Nubia came under EGYPTIAN influence. Southern Nubians, called KUSHITES, grew in power in the 1600s B.C. and again in the 700s B.C.

wall painting showing Nubians presenting gifts

Oo

Olmecs

Olmec figure of a jaguar spirit

The Olmecs of the coast of the Gulf of Mexico created the first known major MESOAMERICAN civilization, between 1500 and 300 B.C. Olmec culture spread north to present-day Mexico and south through Central America. The Olmecs are best known today for huge stone sculptures of human heads and for art with a jaguar design. Whether Olmec influence grew as a result of the wide reach of their trade network, the spread of their religion, or another cause is unknown. After about 800 B.C., their power gradually decreased.

Pp

Parthians

a coin showing the head of a Parthian king

The Parthian Empire lasted from 247 B.C. to A.D. 224 in the region that is now Iran and Afghanistan. Parthians were expert horsemen and archers. They gained wealth through control of trade routes between Europe and Asia. Their empire weakened after several wars with the ROMANS, and they were eventually conquered by the SASSANIANS.

Persians

Persians were nomads who came to the area of what is now Afghanistan and Iran around 1000 B.C. By 550 B.C., they grew to become rulers of a major empire, extending over an area about as large as the United States. It was unified by a system of roads and by a postal system. Persia's contributions to law, government, religion, and art influenced later civilizations, particularly that of the ancient GREEKS. Persian rule ended when Alexander the Great of Macedonia conquered Persia in 333 B.C.

This Persian model chariot, with charioteer and passenger, is made of gold.

Philistine head; part of a coffin lid

Philistines

The Philistines settled a coastal strip of what is now Israel in about 1190 B.C. They may have come from Anatolia (present-day Turkey) and the islands of the Aegean Sea. They were skilled at making things out of iron.

Phoenicians

This seagoing, trading people lived on the coast of what is now Lebanon and parts of Israel and Syria. They came to the area about 3000 B.C. A thousand years later, they began to build cities such as Sidon, Tyre, and Berot (now Beirut). Each city was politically independent of the others, as if it were its own kingdom. Between about 1500 and 500 B.C., northern Phoenicians explored the whole Mediterranean coast, from Asia Minor to Africa. They even reached England and West Africa. Phoenician exports included cedar and pine wood, fine cloth made with rare purple dyes, wine, and glass. Their greatest invention was an alphabet of twenty-two letters, which was adapted by the GREEKS and ROMANS.

Phoenician glass necklace found in an ancient tomb on the Italian island of Sardinia

replica of a Polynesian boat

Polynesians

Polynesians settled a vast, triangular area of islands in the Pacific Ocean, beginning about 2000 B.C. Hawaii, New Zealand, and Easter Island are the three points of the triangle. The Polynesians, who were superb navigators, traveled easily from island to island in double canoes with large sails. Family groups may have gone on seafaring adventures, seeking to start new colonies when their home islands became overcrowded.

The ancient Polynesians made a living from fishing and gardening. Ancient Polynesian craftspeople carved beautiful tools and ship ornaments now housed in museums. The huge stone statues of figures they built on Easter Island have become tourist attractions. Weavers made cloaks and jewelry decorated with feathers. They also wove skirts from the inside bark of plants.

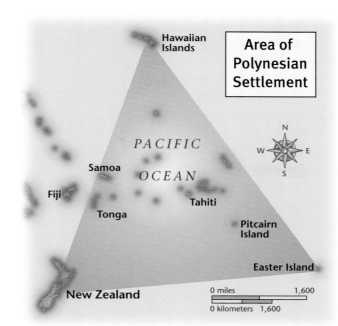

This map shows the triangular area of islands in the Pacific Ocean settled by the Polynesians about 2000 B.C.

From the late sixteenth century onward, colonists and missionaries from Europe and the United States greatly changed Polynesia. They carried many diseases, such as measles and influenza, which killed thousands of Polynesians. Today, Tonga and Western Samoa have kept more of their traditional culture than other parts of Polynesia.

Rr

Romans, Ancient

Key Dates

509 B.C.
ETRUSCAN kings are driven out; the republic is founded.

451 B.C.
The Law of the Twelve Tables, first written code of Roman law, is developed.

About 437–275 B.C.
Rome expands its power throughout the Italian peninsula.

264 B.C.
First war between Rome and Carthage begins.

146 B.C.
Rome destroys Carthage.

A.D. 14
Augustus Caesar, first of eighty Roman emperors, dies.

A.D. 98–180
Emperors Trajan, Hadrian, Antoninus Pius, and Marcus Aurelius expand Rome's power and the idea of providing services for Roman citizens.

A.D. 330
Emperor Constantine establishes second capital at Byzantium, which he later renames Constantinople.

A.D. 476
Rome falls.

The Roman Empire, A.D. 180

ATLANTIC OCEAN
EUROPE
Rome
Black Sea
Byzantium
Pompeii
Athens
Carthage
Sicily
Mediterranean Sea
ASIA
Nile River
N
W E
S
AFRICA
0 miles 1,000
0 kilometers 1,000

From about 509 B.C. to A.D. 476, Roman civilization grew from a small state to a huge empire. Romans set up a republic, or government led by elected officials, in the city of Rome in 509 B.C. This organized government and a strong army enabled Rome to obtain control of all of what is now Italy. After three wars and over a span of 100 years, Rome conquered the north African trading empire of Carthage, in 146 B.C.

The ancient Roman aqueduct at Segovia, Spain, still stands today.

Yet during this time, the republic also had its own civil wars. Toward the end of the civil wars, a great general named Julius Caesar gained power. He was killed one year later, in 44 B.C.

Augustus then took control and defeated all rivals by 31 B.C. to become Rome's first emperor. Rome conquered vast lands held by many different emperors. However, from about A.D. 180, the empire was continually threatened by attack. Rome's long decline took three more centuries, ending in A.D. 476. The eastern part of the empire, however, did survive as the BYZANTINE Empire.

The Roman civilization has continued to influence the modern world. Latin, the language of the Romans, became the basis of a number of languages including Spanish, Portuguese, French, and Italian. Roman architecture has been copied in modern building design. Most important, later builders of democracy have looked to ancient Rome as one model of law and government.

Ss

Sassanians

This dynasty built an empire in present-day Iran, beginning about A.D. 224 with a victory over the PARTHIANS. The Sassanians were themselves overrun by Arab conquerors between A.D. 637 and 651.

Sassanian bowl

Saxons

The Saxons lived in what is now Germany from about the second century A.D. Joined by other Germanic tribes, the Angles and the Jutes, the Saxons invaded England in the fifth and sixth centuries A.D. These groups later became known as the Anglo-Saxons. By the end of the sixth century A.D., the Anglo-Saxons had settled much of present-day England, and had divided into kingdoms. Saxons who remained in Germany battled with the FRANKS and were eventually conquered by them. Saxons in England were conquered by the VIKINGS, but some of their words are still used in the English language.

detail from a Saxon buckle

Scythians

These nomads from central Asia were among the first people to ride horses. After migrating to what is now southern Russia around the seventh century B.C., they built an empire from western Persia to the Egyptian border. In 513 B.C., they fought off an invasion by the PERSIANS. Scythia developed a rich society led by a king and a class of nobles. Their graves were carefully planned and included many fine gold objects.

Scythian sculpture

Siamese

Siamese, or Thai, people established the Sukhothai Kingdom in the twelfth century, in what is now Thailand. Sukhothai, a city-state, expanded into a regional power under King Ramkamhaeng (ruled 1279–1298). Siamese people are known for their architecture, bronzes, and pottery.

The Ho Trai, a scripture library, is one of the most famous architectural structures in Thailand.

traditional Shona huts made of grass and bamboo

Shonas

This group of BANTU people now live in eastern Zimbabwe. Their rule in the area began about 1000. They lived in small villages and made a living by farming. Today, Shonas make up the majority of Zimbabwe's population. Some remain farmers, although others have moved to cities and work in manufacturing and tourism.

decorated box showing a wheeled chariot from the Sumerian city of Ur

Songhai

This empire on the Niger River in Africa grew to power in the fifteenth and sixteenth centuries. Its ruler, Sonni Ali (ruled 1464–1492), captured the Mali capital, Tombouctou. In 1493, a general, Askia Muhammad, seized power and further expanded the empire. The Songhai exported gold and other goods to Arabia and Europe. Tombouctou, a great center of learning under the Songhai, had three major mosques, a university, and 180 schools. After Askia Muhammad was overthrown by his son in 1528, civil wars and rebellions shook the empire. It was conquered by Morocco in 1591.

Songhai coin

Sumerians

The people of Sumer in southern Mesopotamia gave rise to a great civilization around 3500 B.C. Sumerians may have invented wheeled vehicles and the potter's wheel. They invented cuneiform writing and had a rich literature. Because of wars among its city-states, Sumer declined in the 2400s B.C. It was conquered by Sargon of Akkad in the late 2300s B.C. Later, the general Ur-Nammu, who ruled the Sumerian city-state of Ur from 2113 to 2095 B.C., founded a dynasty and developed the Code of Ur-Nammu. This was the world's first known set of laws. Ur fell to the ELAMITES in 2004 B.C., but Sumerian art, architecture, and law influenced the BABYLONIANS.

Tt

Teotihuacános

From about 100 B.C. to A.D. 900, this group of people lived in an area near present-day Mexico City. They developed the largest city in ancient central Mexico, Teotihuacán. It covered an area of 8 square miles. The city included palaces, pyramids, temples, plazas, homes, and a broad main avenue that ran north and south through the city. The city was destroyed sometime between A.D. 650 and 900 by the invading TOLTECS.

Toltec sculpture depicting a warrior

Teotihuacán mask

Toltecs

The Toltecs controlled much of central Mexico from about A.D. 900 to 1187. They originated in the city of Tollan (also called Tula), not far from today's Mexico City. From there they unified several small states into an empire in the late tenth century. Besides having a strong army, the Toltecs were also fine architects, potters, sculptors, and metalworkers. Giant statues, smaller carvings of human and animal figures, serpent columns, and mysterious reclining figures have been found among their ruins. In the twelfth century, they were invaded by several nomadic MESOAMERICAN peoples, including the AZTECS.

Vv

Vikings

Vikings were seafaring peoples of Scandinavia. They conquered different areas of Europe from the ninth to the eleventh centuries A.D. After raiding an area, they often stayed to settle and farm. These fierce warriors were also expert boat builders and active traders.

Danish Vikings took over parts of what is now England, in A.D. 865. They made a truce with the SAXON king of Wessex, Alfred the Great, in A.D. 878, but conflicts continued. Between 1016 and 1042, England was ruled by Denmark's King Canute and his heirs.

Norse, or Norwegian, Vikings raided the Isle of Man and the Scottish isles, as well as what is now Ireland and northwest England. They settled Iceland beginning about A.D. 900. They colonized Greenland under Eric the Red. His son, Leif Eriksson, most likely traveled to North America in 1002.

Swedish Vikings went east of the Baltic Sea, entering the cities of Kiev, in present-day Ukraine and Novgorod in what is today Russia.

They ruled over and were assimilated into the local Slavic population. The Swedish Vikings were called the Rus by Greek and Arab traders. The Slavs, whom the Rus ruled, took that name and called their land Russia.

Viking memorial showing a Viking longboat

Glossary

adobe   brick made of sun-dried clay and straw

artifacts   tools, weapons, or other simple objects used in ancient times that have survived through to today

assimilated   mixed with and became part of another culture

city-states   cities that are independent political states

culture   a people's way of life, including customs, beliefs, and language

cuneiform   a system of writing featuring wedge-shaped notches in clay, probably invented by the Sumerians

dynasty   a line of rulers descended from one another

fresco   a painting made on damp plastered walls or ceilings

hieroglyphs   writing in which pictures represent words or sounds

irrigate   to use channels dug by people to supply water to crops

maize   a type of cereal crop; corn

monotheistic   worshiping a single god

nomads   people who change their dwelling place frequently as they move in search of food and water

pyramid   a large structure with four sloping triangular sides rising from a rectangular base, used as a tomb or temple

successors   people who follow in a position, title, or office

wampum   small beads made of shells that were used by Native Americans as money or as decoration

wigwams   dome-shaped dwellings made with a pole frame covered with bark or skins, used by Native American peoples in the eastern United States